Journey Eight

A collection of images from Travel Photographer of the Year

Travel Photographer of the Year Ltd - The Photographers' Press

Publisher/Editor/Author - Chris Coe
Editor - Karen Coe
Designer - Gabrielle Davies

First published by Travel Photographer of the Year Ltd,
20 Yew Tree Courtyard, Earl Soham, Suffolk IP13 7SG, UK
www.tpoty.com

First edition published in July 2016
ISBN: 978-0-9549396-8-7

Reproduced, printed and bound by:
DLM Creative, Suite S1 Audley House, Northbridge Road, Berkhamsted, HP4 1EH.

Front cover photograph: Inner Mongolia, China. **Cai Zhiping,** China.

Frontispiece photograph: Dundret nature reserve, Swedish Lapland. **Gunar Streu,** Germany.

Page 3 photograph: Tindari Monastery, Patti, Sicily, Italy. **Piers Golden,** UK.

Page 4 photograph: United States Navy DC-3 on Sólheimasandur, Iceland. **Trevor Cole,** UK.

Page 5 photograph: Foundation School, Gilgit-Baltistan, northern Pakistan.
Andrea Francolini, Italy.

Back cover photograph (top left): Maramures, Romania. **Mitchell Kanashkevich,** Australia.

Back cover photograph (middle left): Near Ilulissat, Disko Bay, Greenland.
Stephan Fürnrohr, Germany.

Back cover photograph (bottom left): Atchafalaya Basin, Louisiana, USA.
Marsel van Oosten, Netherlands.

Back cover photograph (middle right): Heligoland, North Sea. **Uli Kunz,** Germany.

CONTENTS

Introduction	4
Travel Photographer of the Year	6
Young Travel Photographer of the Year	12
Faces, People, Encounters Portfolio	24
Nature & Environment Portfolio	34
Monochromal Portfolio	44
One Shot – A Moment in Light	54
One Shot – Colours of the World	60
One Shot – Water	66
New Talent – Street Culture	70
Smart Shot – iCaptured	80
Best Single Image in a Portfolio	84
Judges	101
Sponsors and Partners	103
Index of Photographers	107
Travel Photographer of the Year Collection	108

Since launching Travel Photographer of the Year in 2003, it has been one of our objectives to broaden people's perception of travel photography. Unlike other areas of photography, it is not a single genre. Travel encompasses many interests and activities and travel photography reflects this.

Journey Eight contains images from the 13th awards, and in those 13 years the Journey books have featured a remarkable diversity of imagery, both in subject matter and style. This is a reflection of the challenging themes which the awards have set, but also of the many and talented photographers who shoot travel images in a myriad of different ways, unconstrained by what publishers will reproduce and for the love of both photography and travel.

In terms of making a living, travel photography is both a dream job and a nightmare. Yet it may be for these very reasons that it inspires creativity and we are seeing such diversity, with photographers following their creative instincts rather than being limited to shooting what has commercial value. For those of us who travel and take photographs for fun then this was always the way of things.

Looking back over the years the diversity is certainly evident. Not just colour versus black and white, but in theme and style too. Travel photography draws on a spectrum of styles from reportage to fine art, and on photographic genres from people, landscape, wildlife, architecture, food and drink, places and history… the list goes on, and all of these feature across the eight Journey portfolio books.

One of the problems with photography is that pictures are now most commonly viewed online and at low resolution. This works for some images but often the subtle ones lose out. The TPOTY exhibitions provide the chance to see these glorious images up close and personal in a larger format. As the exhibitions tour this affords the opportunity to revisit some of the great images from previous years as well as exploring the new ones, reinforcing the diversity of imagery and the skills of travel photography's best exponents.

It's uplifting and inspiring, reinforcing the fact that great photography doesn't just happen because you have a camera or a smartphone. Like any skill, it improves with time and practice. For those lucky enough to have an innate eye for light and composition it is obviously more natural but photography is inclusive. We can all take a great image, we all have one in us. Sometimes luck and 'right place, right time' are the key components but that doesn't matter. *Making* a great image takes more. Just like playing an instrument, crafting a melody takes practice and skill. Making, crafting an image takes practice and a deeper understanding of subject, light and composition.

Most of all, when we achieve this through whatever combination of luck and skill, the end result has impact. It can move, enchant, repulse or inspire the viewer but nonetheless it has an impact. It becomes memorable and touches our emotions.

As we travel, as the travel experience inspires us, photography allows us to share this inspiration with those who weren't there. In capturing moments well, we capture the senses – sight obviously, but also sounds, smells, tastes, textures. In doing so the mundane and the ordinary meet with the unusual and the different to expand our world and our perception of others. Now travel to the next page and be inspired!

TRAVEL PHOTOGRAPHER
OF THE YEAR 2015

 Pelicans at sea and a Louisiana swamp in black and white make two powerful portfolios. Marsel van Oosten's winning images showcase both subjects elegantly. They are beautifully composed and show wonderful use of light, with the black and white medium only serving to enhance their impact.

The first portfolio of the cypress trees in the Atchafalaya Basin, Louisiana, USA, is subtle and textural, contrasting with the strong, punchy, graphic style of the portfolio of great white pelicans, shot on a boat in the Atlantic Ocean near Walvis Bay, Namibia. The detail in both portfolios makes them intriguing and captivating.

Sponsors of this award:
TPOTY, Plastic Sandwich

Atlantic Ocean, Walvis Bay, Namibia. **Marsel van Oosten, Netherlands.** *Nikon D810, 24-70mm lens, f16, 1/400s, ISO 160*

Atlantic Ocean, Walvis Bay, Namibia. **Marsel van Oosten, Netherlands.** *Nikon D810, 24-70mm lens, f11, 1/2000s, ISO 400*

TRAVEL PHOTOGRAPHER
OF THE YEAR 2015

Marsel van Oosten Netherlands
Winner

These two great white pelicans landed on our boat, allowing me to get some good close-up shots. I really liked the repetition of the shapes, but when the foreground pelican opened its beak, that really took it to the next level.

It's quite rare to see a pelican close-up taken with a wide-angle lens, so that's what I wanted to try here. One of the great things about shooting with a wide-angle is the distorted perspective, which creates very dynamic shapes and lines.

Atlantic Ocean, Walvis Bay, Namibia. **Marsel van Oosten, Netherlands.** *Nikon D810, 24-70mm lens, f16, 1/800s, ISO 400*

Atlantic Ocean, Walvis Bay, Namibia. **Marsel van Oosten, Netherlands.** *Nikon D810, 24-70mm lens, f16, 1/500s, ISO 200*

TRAVEL PHOTOGRAPHER
OF THE YEAR 2015

Marsel van Oosten Netherlands
Winner

In my photography graphic shapes and lines are very important, and so is the
absence of clutter. However, the swamps in Louisiana are exactly that: clutter. Yet
this was actually a good reason for me to go there. From a creative point of view
it's important to step outside of your comfort zone every now and then.

Atchafalaya Basin, Louisiana, USA. **Marsel van Oosten, Netherlands.** *Nikon D4, 80-400mm lens, f16, 1/400s, ISO 200*

The decision to do an entire series in black and white was very counter-intuitive, because the colours in autumn here can be quite stunning. But colour is both the easy and obvious choice – mostly because people respond very well to bright and saturated colours – and colour can be very distracting. Good black and white photography is way harder than colour, because you don't have those catchy colours to help you. Light, contrast, texture, shapes, and composition need to be spot on or the shot won't work.

I'm always looking for ways to do things differently than other photographers, so I decided to include people, in this case my wife Daniella, in my shots. A person in the landscape will bring that landscape to life, it will add a sense of adventure, and it will give a sense of scale.

Atchafalaya Basin, Louisiana, USA. **Marsel van Oosten, Netherlands.**
Nikon D810, 70-200mm lens, f16, 1/160s, ISO 800

Atchafalaya Basin, Louisiana, USA. **Marsel van Oosten, Netherlands.**
Nikon D810, 70-200mm lens, f16, 1/200s, ISO 400

Atchafalaya Basin, Louisiana, USA. **Marsel van Oosten, Netherlands.**
Nikon D4, 80-400mm lens, f18, 1/250s, ISO 200

YOUNG TRAVEL PHOTOGRAPHER OF THE YEAR 2015

 This set of reportage images gets beneath the skin of life for the Basotho people in Semonkong, Lesotho. Much more than just snaps, Chase Guttman's portraits illuminate the character of these people, linking their lives to the landscapes which surround them and linking them with the subtle blue tones running through the portfolio.

Sponsors of this award:

Photo Iconic, Plastic Sandwich, TPOTY

Semonkong, Lesotho. **Chase Guttman, USA (age 18).** *Nikon D7000, 12-24mm lens, f9, 1/320s, ISO 100*

YOUNG TRAVEL PHOTOGRAPHER OF THE YEAR 2015

Chase Guttman USA
Winner

Semonkong, Lesotho. **Chase Guttman, USA (age 18).** *Nikon D7000, 12-24mm lens, f4, 1/30s, ISO 100*

Page 13: High in the 'Kingdom of the Sky', Basotho ponies are lovingly cared for by local Sotho tribes who are reliant on these animals to traverse the harsh and mountainous terrain.

Left: Shepherds, donning balaclava-like masks, converge on the jagged basalt cliffs of Maletsunyane Falls as the sun begins to rise.

Right: In the frost-laden foothills of the remote nation of Lesotho, the Basotho people wear traditional tribal blankets for village ceremonies and familial milestones.

Below right: A mother's home cooked meal warms the interior of a mud hut where a young child affectionately embraces her parent.

Semonkong, Lesotho. **Chase Guttman, USA (age 18).** *Nikon D7000, 12-24mm lens, f4, 1/50s, ISO 800*

Semonkong, Lesotho. **Chase Guttman, USA (age 18).** *Nikon D7000, 12-24mm lens, f4, 1/30s, ISO 800*

Jökulsárlón beach, Iceland. **Spencer Cox, USA (age 18).** *Nikon D800E, 24mm lens, f16, 0.6s, ISO 100*

YOUNG TRAVEL PHOTOGRAPHER OF THE YEAR 2015

Spencer Cox USA
Winner - 15-18 age group

Left: Iceland is home to Jökulsárlón, one of the most spectacular beaches in the world. Here, hundreds of icebergs from a nearby glacier wash ashore onto a black sand beach. The crystal colour of this particular iceberg struck me, and the dramatic blue sky provided a perfect backdrop.

Right: I took this photograph on one of the windiest days of my life. The drama in the dark-blue sky was matched by the fierce ocean. It was one of the most intense mornings I had ever seen.

Below left: Due to Iceland's position at the edge of the Arctic Circle, the sun barely sets during the middle of summer. I took this photograph a bit after midnight.

Below right: This sunset was perhaps the most beautiful hour of lighting of my life.

Stokksnes Mountains, Iceland. **Spencer Cox, USA (age 18).** *Nikon D800E, 24mm lens, f16, 8s, ISO 100*

Jökulsárlón Glacier Lagoon, Iceland. **Spencer Cox, USA (age 18).** *Nikon D800E, 105mm lens, f7.1, 1/3s, ISO 100*

Höfn, Iceland. **Spencer Cox, USA (age 18).** *Nikon D800E, 24mm lens, f16, 1/3s, ISO 100*

Shinjuku, Tokyo, Japan. **Jonathan Rystrøm, Denmark (age 16).** *Canon EOS 60D, 24-105mm lens, f4, 1/100s, ISO 3200*

Shinjuku, Tokyo, Japan. **Jonathan Rystrøm, Denmark (age 16).**
Canon EOS 60D, 24-105mm lens, f4.5, 1/15s, ISO 1250

YOUNG TRAVEL PHOTOGRAPHER OF THE YEAR 2015

Jonathan Rystrøm Denmark
Runner Up - 15-18 age group

Above: Even in the rain, the young Japanese never miss a chance to check their smartphones.

Left: A young woman is checking her phone on her way from Shinjuku, the world's largest train station.

Shinjuku, Tokyo, Japan. **Jonathan Rystrøm, Denmark (age 16).** *Canon EOS 60D, 24-105mm lens, f4, 1/30s, ISO 3200*

Above: Rain is no barrier for taking photos in busy Tokyo. Even when the person being photographed would rather be seeking dry shelter.

Left: When the rain strikes Tokyo, umbrellas are rushed out quicker than you can say 'sushi'!

Shinjuku, Tokyo, Japan. **Jonathan Rystrøm, Denmark (age 16).**
Canon EOS 60D, 24-105mm lens, f4, 1/160s, ISO 1000

YOUNG TRAVEL PHOTOGRAPHER OF THE YEAR 2015

Michael Theodric Indonesia
Winner - 14 and under age group

The Cioko (Hungry Ghost Festival) ceremony. It is believed that souls who have not received offerings or prayers from their families are 'hungry', so this festival is held to 'feed' them and ward off evil.

Boen San Bio Temple, Tangerang, Indonesia. **Michael Theodric, Indonesia (age 13).**
Canon EOS 5D MkII, 17-40mm lens, f4, 1/60s, ISO 4000

Boen San Bio Temple, Tangerang, Indonesia. **Michael Theodric, Indonesia (age 13).** *Canon EOS 5D MkII, 17-40mm lens, f4, 1/50s, ISO 4000*

Boen San Bio Temple, Tangerang, Indonesia. **Michael Theodric, Indonesia (age 13).** *Canon EOS 5D MkII, 17-40mm lens, f4, 1/30s, ISO 4000*

Top: Burning a 6m tall paper statue during the Cioko. It is believed that, by burning these statues, disaster will be averted.

Right: Teenagers performing the Lion Dance during the Cioko.

Boen San Bio Temple, Tangerang, Indonesia. **Michael Theodric, Indonesia (age 13).** *Canon EOS 5D MkII, 17-40mm lens, f4, 1/15s, ISO 4000*

YOUNG TRAVEL PHOTOGRAPHER OF THE YEAR 2015

Victor Ghose UK
Runner Up - 14 and under age group

My family travelled to Canada for a wedding, and we spent a few days in Cape Breton in Nova Scotia, visiting the beautiful old UNESCO city of Lunenberg and the pretty village of Baddeck.

Baddeck, Nova Scotia, Canada. **Victor Ghose UK (age 8).**
Canon Power Shot SX50HS, f5, 1/125s, ISO 80

Lunenburg, Nova Scotia, Canada. **Victor Ghose UK (age 8).**
Canon Power Shot SX50HS, f5, 1/1000s, ISO 320

Lunenburg, Nova Scotia, Canada. **Victor Ghose UK (age 8).**
Canon Power Shot SX50HS, f4.5, 1/1000s, ISO 100

Baddeck, Nova Scotia, Canada. **Victor Ghose UK (age 8).**
Canon Power Shot SX50HS, f5.6, 1/400s, ISO 800

Hula Valley, Israel. **Ido Scharf, Israel (age 16).** *Olympus OM-D E-M5, 75-300mm lens, f6.7, 1/3200s, ISO 16*

YOUNG TRAVEL PHOTOGRAPHER OF THE YEAR 2015

Ido Scharf Israel
Special Mention - 15-18 age group

Two cranes flying over Hula Valley, forming a heart shape.

YOUNG TRAVEL PHOTOGRAPHER OF THE YEAR 2015

Hugo Berman France
Special Mention - 14 and under age group

This sadhu didn't see me taking the picture so, fortunately, he didn't pose. (Image taken from portfolio.)

Kathmandu, Nepal. **Hugo Berman, France (age 11).** *Canon EOS Rebel T3i, 18-200mm lens, f6.3, 1/250s, ISO 100*

FACES, PEOPLE, ENCOUNTERS
PORTFOLIO 2015

Mitchell Kanashkevich's portfolio cleverly tells an intimate story of life in Maramures, Romania. The images have a subtle, textural almost painterly quality. Beautifully composed in soft natural light, they invite us into a different world.

Sponsor of this award:
Direct Photographic

Maramures, Romania. **Mitchell Kanashkevich, Australia.** *Canon EOS 5D MkII, 20mm lens, f3.2, 1/50s, ISO 800*

Maramures, Romania. **Mitchell Kanashkevich, Australia.** *Canon EOS 5D MkII, 24-70mm lens, f4.5, 1/400s, ISO 400*

FACES, PEOPLE, ENCOUNTERS
PORTFOLIO 2015

Mitchell Kanashkevich Australia
Winner

Previous page: Rural Romanian woman preparing pumpkins for winter.

Opposite page: A shepherd herding the village's animals atop a hill.

Right: Farmer taking a break from tilling the fields before winter.

Below right: Elderly man making Tuică in a traditional alcohol-making machine.

Maramures, Romania. **Mitchell Kanashkevich, Australia.** *Canon EOS 5D MkII, 24-70mm lens, f3.2, 1/640s, ISO 200*

Maramures, Romania. **Mitchell Kanashkevich, Australia.** *Canon EOS 5D MkII, 24-70mm lens, f3.2, 1/320s, ISO 400*

FACES, PEOPLE, ENCOUNTERS
PORTFOLIO 2015

Timothy Allen UK
Runner Up

During the summer months in the Altai Mountains of Western Mongolia, weddings are a daily occurrence. Kazakh nomadic weddings involve a marriage ceremony and the obligatory wedding DJ but also horse racing, a wrestling tournament and copious amounts of prepared food and drink served in the families' gers.

Western Mongolia. **Timothy Allen, UK.** *Canon 5D MkII, 16-35mm lens, f2.8, 1/80s, ISO 640*

Western Mongolia. **Timothy Allen, UK.** *Canon 5D MkII, 16-35mm lens, f2.8, 1/160s, ISO 640*

Western Mongolia. **Timothy Allen, UK.**
Canon 5D MkII, 16-35mm lens, f9, 1/2000s, ISO 640

Western Mongolia. **Timothy Allen, UK.**
Canon 5D MkII, 50mm lens, f1.2, 1/8000s, ISO 100

Nunnery near Yangon, Myanmar. **Sue O'Connell, UK.** *Canon EOS 6D, 24-105mm lens, f5, 1/500s, ISO 640*

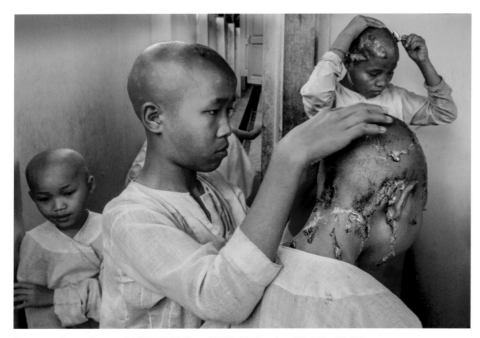

Nunnery near Yangon, Myanmar. **Sue O'Connell, UK.** Canon EOS 6D, 16-35mm lens, f11, 1/80s, ISO 800

FACES, PEOPLE, ENCOUNTERS
PORTFOLIO 2015

Sue O'Connell UK
Highly Commended

Right: The youngest echelon of novices fresh from their morning lessons. These girls, most likely refugees from war zones or poverty, have found sanctuary here.

Below: Lunchtime at the nunnery - the single main meal of the day and another ritual whose various stages, from preparation through eating to washing up, are carried out with great discipline.

Left: It may be monsoon season but life in the nunnery must go on. The younger inmates are temporarily stranded by the ferocity of the downpour but fortune favours the brave as some older novices make a dash for it.

Below left: Head shaving is one of the routines that punctuates the life of the nunnery. It is a ritual carried out with great efficiency.

Nunnery near Yangon, Myanmar. **Sue O'Connell, UK.** *Canon EOS 6D, 16-35mm lens, f5.6, 1/125s, ISO 800*

Nunnery near Yangon, Myanmar. **Sue O'Connell, UK.** *Canon EOS 6D, 16-35mm lens, f6.3, 1/60s, ISO 400*

Simbai, Papua New Guinea. **Stuart Redler, UK.** *Leica S2, 120mm lens, f2.5, 1/250s, ISO 640*

Simbai, Papua New Guinea. **Stuart Redler, UK.** *Leica S2, 30-90mm lens, f8, 1/30s, ISO 640*

FACES, PEOPLE, ENCOUNTERS
PORTFOLIO 2015

Stuart Redler UK
Commended

Above: Child wearing a headdress made of bird feathers and a necklace made of woven cane rings looped together.

Left: Man from the Kalam tribe wearing a necklace made of hornbill beaks and decorated with beads and vegetation.

Middle Sepik, Papua New Guinea. **Stuart Redler, UK.** *Leica S2, 120mm lens, f4, 1/125s, ISO 320*

Tufi, Papua New Guinea. **Stuart Redler, UK.** *Leica S2, 30-90mm lens, f8, 1/500s, ISO 640*

Above: The Chambri tribe, who live along the Sepik river in Papua New Guinea, believe crocodiles emerged from the river and became humans. Male members of the tribe undergo an initiation ceremony, which involves cutting the skin multiple times to resemble crocodile scales.

Left: A canoeist wears traditional decorations made of dried palm leaves.

NATURE & ENVIRONMENT PORTFOLIO 2015

The natural world can be a harsh place, with man playing a role in the natural order of hunter and hunted. James Morgan's portfolio on wolf hunters in Yakutia, Russia captures a very powerful interaction between man and nature in a bleak environment. Striking, brutal and graphic as it is, it is also intimate and captivating.

Sponsor of this award:
TPOTY

Yakutia, Russia. **James Morgan, UK.** *Canon EOS 1D C, 11-24mm lens, f4, 1/250s, ISO 125*

Yakutia, Russia. **James Morgan, UK.** *Canon EOS 5D MkII, 11-24mm lens, f4, 1/400s, ISO 200*

NATURE & ENVIRONMENT
PORTFOLIO 2015

James Morgan UK
Winner

Previous page: Ion Maxsimovic demonstrates how to set a trap. Hunting with these traps was banned in an agreement signed in 2008 by Russia, Canada and the EU. But as wolf numbers soared, hunters in Siberia began to use them again for lack of a humane alternative.

Above: The hunter holds up the head of the wolf he has just shot dead. In winter an adult male will freeze solid within two hours of death.

Left: Yegor Dyachkovsky adds wood to the pile while Ion Maxsimovic douses it with petrol. Hunters are paid for every wolf skin they deliver, but the carcasses are burned.

Below: Ion Maxsimovic watches as the latest wolf carcass is burned. Ion is one of Siberia's most successful hunters. In 2013 he was awarded a substantial cash prize for delivering the most wolf pelts.

Yakutia, Russia. **James Morgan, UK.**
Canon EOS 1D C, 11-24mm lens, f4, 1/320s, ISO 320

Yakutia, Russia. **James Morgan, UK.** *Canon EOS 1D C, 70-200mm lens, f4, 1/320s, ISO 250*

NATURE & ENVIRONMENT
PORTFOLIO 2015

Francisco Mingorance Spain
Runner Up

Río Tinto, Huelva, Andalucía, Spain. **Francisco Mingorance, Spain.** *Canon EOS-1D X, 70-200mm lens, f5.6, 1/2000s, ISO 500*

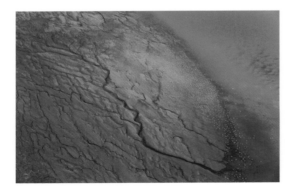

Río Tinto, Huelva, Andalucía, Spain. **Francisco Mingorance, Spain.** *Canon EOS-1D X, 70-200mm lens, f5.6, 1/1000s, ISO 500*

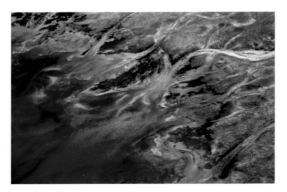

Río Tinto, Huelva, Andalucía, Spain. **Francisco Mingorance, Spain.** *Canon EOS-1D X, 70-200mm lens, f4.5, 1/2000s, ISO 500*

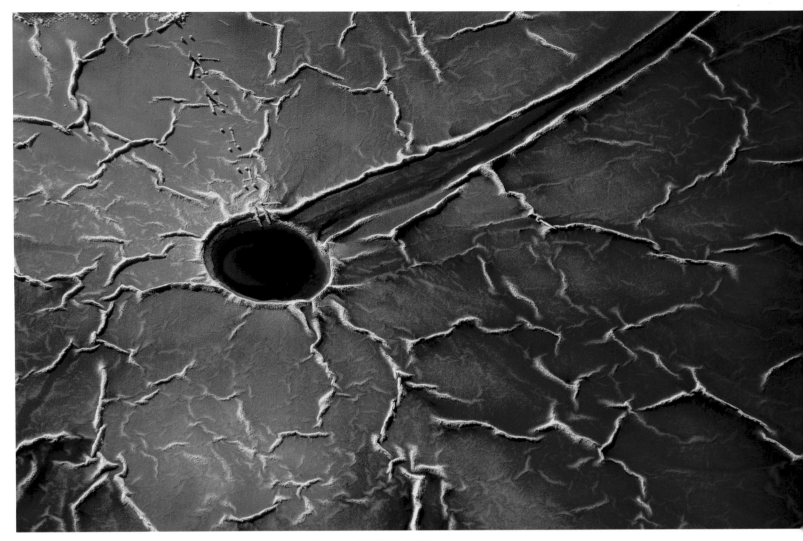

Río Tinto, Huelva, Andalucía, Spain. **Francisco Mingorance, Spain.** *Canon EOS-1D X, 70-200mm lens, f5.6, 1/800s, ISO 500*

Opposite page above: The waters lapping against the red tones of the land create striking engravings - reminiscent of a group of small trees - carved in the mud.

Opposite page below left: A large group of seagulls concentrated on the edge of the delta. Because of the acidity of the water, it is very unusual to see birds in Rio Tinto.

Opposite page below right: The river's name comes from the reddish ochre of its banks. These colours are due to the high concentrates of ferruginous salts and ferric sulphates which have existed here since the dawn of history.

Above: The radioactive discharge from the phosphogypsum ponds has destroyed part of the red marsh. This view caught my attention on a low-flying training session, because of its resemblance to the impact of an asteroid on the green waters.

NATURE & ENVIRONMENT
PORTFOLIO 2015

Ingrid Vekemans Belgium
Highly Commended

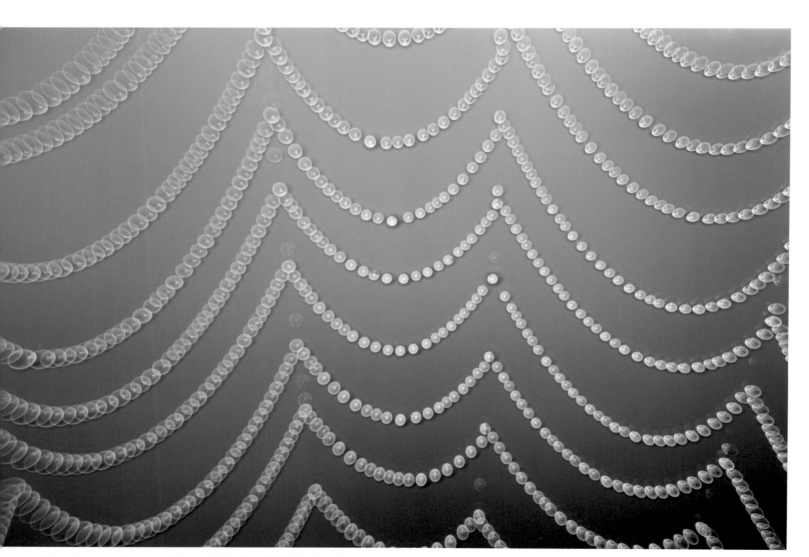

Torfbroek, Kampenhout, Belgium. **Ingrid Vekemans, Belgium.** *Nikon D800E, 50mm lens, f1.8, 1/1250s, ISO 50*

Torfbroek, Kampenhout, Belgium. **Ingrid Vekemans, Belgium.**
Nikon D800E, 50mm lens, f1.8, 1/2000s, ISO 50

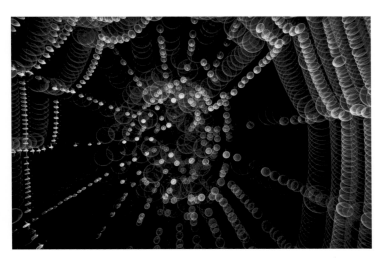

Torfbroek, Kampenhout, Belgium. **Ingrid Vekemans, Belgium.**
Nikon D800E, 50mm lens, f1.8, 1/800s, ISO 100

Torfbroek, Kampenhout, Belgium. **Ingrid Vekemans, Belgium.**
Nikon D800E, 50mm lens, f1.8, 1/6400s, ISO 100

Dewy mornings always invite me to go for the 50mm lens fully open, using extension tubes to create an exuberant bokeh in the dew drops, back-lit by the rising sun. I have used this on several subjects, this time it was spiders' webs, shot with double exposure in camera.

Nanchang, Jiangxi, China. **Jianhui Liao, China.** *Nikon D4, 600mm lens, f4.5, 1/2000s, ISO 100*

Nanchang, Jiangxi, China. **Jianhui Liao, China.** *Nikon D4, 600mm lens, f4, 1/250s, ISO 100*

Nanchang, Jiangxi, China. **Jianhui Liao, China.**
Nikon D4, 600mm lens, f4.5, 1/320s, ISO 100

NATURE & ENVIRONMENT
PORTFOLIO 2015

Jianhui Liao China
Commended

Every year, hundreds of thousands of egrets gather in the Xiangshan Forest Park to breed. 12 out of the world's 15 different species of egrets can be seen in a magnificent spectacle here.

Nanchang, Jiangxi, China. **Jianhui Liao, China.** *Nikon D4, 600mm lens, f4.5, 1/3200s, ISO 100*

MONOCHROMAL PORTFOLIO 2015

Black and white photography has an enduring presence and appeal to photographers. It showcases the key elements of photography and composition.

Although boat towing is no longer a necessity, it was once a way of life and the only way to negotiate this section of rapids in Hubei, China. Xia Xuejun has captured the ancient activity with humour in a striking portfolio of strongly composed images, much stronger for being shot in black and white and without the distraction of colour.

Sponsor of this award:

StaaG

Hubei, China. **Xia Xuejun, China.** *Canon EOS 1DX, 16-35mm lens, f13, 1/125s, ISO 100*

Hubei, China. **Xia Xuejun, China.** *Canon EOS 1DX, 16-35mm lens, f8, 1/20s, ISO 100*

Hubei, China. **Xia Xuejun, China.** *Nikon D800, 24-70mm lens, f9, 1/320s, ISO 100*

MONOCHROMAL
PORTFOLIO 2015

Xia Xuejun China
Winner

Boat tracking, towing boats by human power, was once the norm in this region, even as recently as the 1950s. Traditionally the trackers were poor farmers, who supplemented their income by towing boats. They would do this naked, to prevent their clothes from getting wet.

The gentleman with the goatee is Mr.Xiang Wenbing, who worked his whole life as a boat tracker. He recently died at the age of 83.

Today, with the region now accessible by road, the traditional activity is staged generally as a tourist attraction and most of the trackers lost their jobs.

Hubei, China. **Xia Xuejun, China.** *Nikon D800, 24-70mm lens, f10, 1/200s, ISO 100*

Galapagos Islands, Ecuador. **Philip Lee Harvey, UK.**
Canon EOS 1DX, 70-200mm lens, f4.5, 1/320s, ISO 640

Galapagos Islands, Ecuador. **Philip Lee Harvey, UK.**
Canon EOS 1DX, 70-200mm lens, f4, 1/400s, ISO 400

MONOCHROMAL
PORTFOLIO 2015

Philip Lee Harvey UK
Runner Up

Above: Salty Lightfoot crab on North Seymour Island.

Above right: Galapagos sea lion in the evening light.

Below right: Giant tortoise, approximately 100 years old.

Opposite page: Marine Iguanas basking in the evening sun.

Galapagos Islands, Ecuador. **Philip Lee Harvey, UK.** *Canon EOS 1DX, 70-200mm lens, f5, 1/125s, ISO 800*

Galapagos Islands, Ecuador. **Philip Lee Harvey, UK.** *Canon EOS 1DX, 70-200mm lens, f5.6, 1/400s, ISO 200*

MONOCHROMAL
PORTFOLIO 2015

Larry Louie Cananda
Highly Commended

Dhaka, Bangladesh. **Larry Louie, Canada.** *Canon EOS 5D MkII, 24-105mm lens, f6.3, 1/80s, ISO 1600*

Dhaka, Bangladesh. **Larry Louie, Canada.** *Canon EOS 5D MkII, 24-105mm lens, f4, 1/125s, ISO 800*

Dhaka, Bangladesh. **Larry Louie, Canada.** *Canon EOS 5D MkII, 24-105mm lens, f2.2, 1/125s, ISO 1000*

Dhaka, Bangladesh. **Larry Louie, Canada.** *Canon EOS 5D MkII, 24-105mm lens, f10, 1/125s, ISO 1600*

Stepping into the Hazaribagh neighbourhood in Dhaka, Bangladesh is like stepping back in time. This tannery district has not changed for many years. They still operate as they did 100 years ago, with little technology or machinery.

There are about 200 tanneries that sell to international fashion labels. The tanning industry in the heart of Bangladesh's capital is booming.

MONOCHROMAL
PORTFOLIO 2015

Adam Tan Malaysia
Commended

Hangzhou, China. **Adam Tan, Malaysia.** *Nikon D800, 24-70mm lens, f9, 30s, ISO 100*

Hangzhou, China. **Adam Tan, Malaysia.** *Nikon D800, 24-70mm lens, f9, 191s, ISO 500*

Hangzhou, China. **Adam Tan, Malaysia.**
Nikon D800, 24-70mm lens, f7.1, 482s, ISO 400

West Lake in early Spring. I used 10EV and 6EV neutral density filters to achieve the effect of a fusion of traditional Chinese painting and contemporary minimalist B&W fine art techniques.

Hangzhou, China. **Adam Tan, Malaysia.** *Nikon D800, 24-70mm lens, f8, 30s, ISO 200*

ONE SHOT 2015
A MOMENT IN LIGHT

Whilst photography has the power to freeze a moment in time, great photography captures that moment and makes it memorable.

Uli Kunz's wonderful winning image, shot in Heligoland, captures a fleeting moment and sculpts it into a powerful, dynamic, graphic and cleverly conceived photograph. Light and shadow create an eerie image which is none the less striking for that slightly sinister feel.

Sponsor of this award:
Photo Iconic

Heligoland, North Sea. **Uli Kunz, Germany.** *Sony A7S, 16mm lens, f9, 1/5s, ISO 4000*

ONE SHOT 2015
A MOMENT IN LIGHT

Uli Kunz Germany
Winner

Previous page: In the darkness, the light rays of the powerful lighthouse on top of the island cast moving shadows on the walls, which gave me the idea for this picture.

ONE SHOT 2015
A MOMENT IN LIGHT

David Wrangborg Sweden
Runner Up

Below: The polar light has broken through the clouds and is playing along the coast of Isfjorden on Svalbard.

Blomster Høgda, Svalbard, Norway. **David Wrangborg, Sweden.** *Pentax K5, 55-300mm lens, f8, 1/20s, ISO 100*

South East Ridge of Makalu, Himalaya, Nepal. **Tim Taylor, UK.** *Canon EOS 5D MkIII, 24-70mm lens, f22, 1/250s, ISO 200*

ONE SHOT 2015
A MOMENT IN LIGHT

Tim Taylor UK
Highly Commended

Above: At 22,000ft above sea level, the weather is everything; making the wrong choices can cost you your life.

Dundret nature reserve, Swedish Lapland. **Gunar Streu, Germany.** *Nikon D810, 24-70mm lens, f2.8, 20s, ISO 400*

ONE SHOT 2015
A MOMENT IN LIGHT

Gunar Streu Germany
Commended

Hoarfrost-covered cabin at dusk, with Northern
Lights in the background.

ONE SHOT 2015
A MOMENT IN LIGHT

Cai Zhiping China
Commended

On winter mornings when the prairie turns white, a group of horses galloping down the mountain forms a magnificent scroll on the snowy grassland.

Inner Mongolia, China. **Cai Zhiping, China.** *Canon EOS 1D MkIV, 100-400mm lens, f3, 1/800s, ISO 400*

ONE SHOT 2015
COLOURS OF THE WORLD

Colour can transform, mask or illuminate. It makes our world vibrant, regardless of whether it is vivid or subtle, saturated or pastel.

Prayer flags are much photographed but rarely as well as these. Larry Louie's image is moody with both weather-worn pastel tones and movement giving a real sense of place in the Tibetan Tagong grasslands.

Sponsor of this award:
Photo Iconic

Tibetan Tagong grasslands, Sichuan, China. **Larry Louie, Canada.** *Canon EOS 5D Mk II, 24-105mm lens, f14, 1s, ISO 100*

Tindari Monastery, Patti, Sicily, Italy. **Piers Golden, UK.** *Fujifilm 645i, 60mm lens, f8, 1/1000s, ISO 100*

ONE SHOT 2015
COLOURS OF THE WORLD

Larry Louie Canada
Winner

Previous page. Tibetan prayer flags are religious vessels carrying silent prayers of blessings. The wind, the breath of Nature, activates, dissolves and carries the spiritual vibration of the ancient Buddhist prayers, mantras and powerful symbols displayed on the flags.

ONE SHOT 2015
COLOURS OF THE WORLD

Piers Golden UK
Runner Up

Left. A Blue Nun stands and looks out from the promontory high above the Tyrrhenian Sea. Tindari Monastery is home to the Black Madonna, Santa Maria of Tindari.

ONE SHOT 2015
COLOURS OF THE WORLD

Ignacio Palacios Spain/Australia
Highly Commended

Opposite page. In September there are normally a lot of flamingos and other birds in the area and this gives another dimension to the already beautiful patterns and textures that can be photographed from the air.

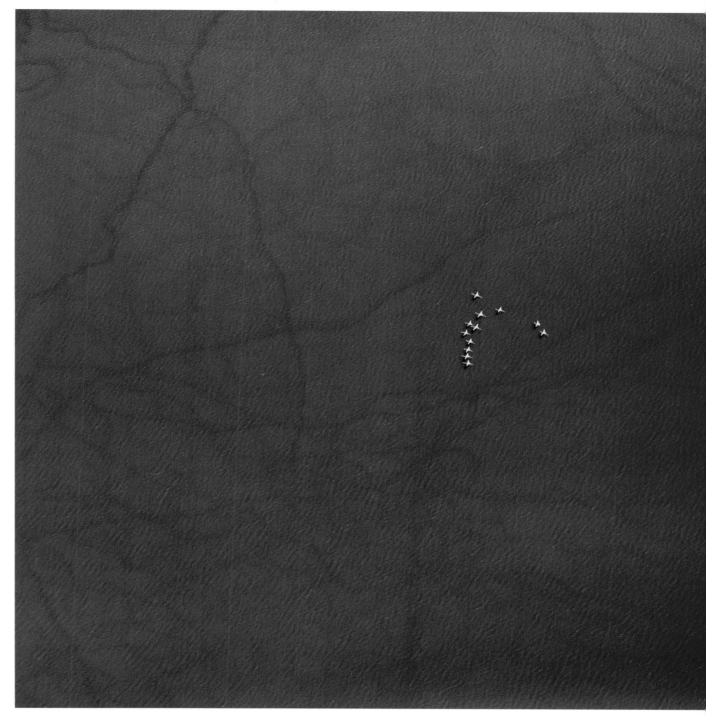

Marismas del Guadalquivir, Andalucia, Spain. **Ignacio Palacios, Spain/Australia.** *Nikon D600, 70-200mm lens, f4.5, 1/4000s, ISO 800*

Sichuan province, China. **Zhou Jianyong, China.** *Nikon D3S, f5.6, 1/125s, ISO 200*

ONE SHOT 2015
COLOURS OF THE WORLD

Zhou Jianyong China
Commended

Sichuan is one of the most populated provinces in China. On scorching summer days, people come to the pool to get away from the heat.

ONE SHOT 2015
COLOURS OF THE WORLD

Maria de la Guardia USA
Commended

Afghan women are often unable to secure jobs for cultural reasons, a situation made more difficult by high rates of illiteracy. Here they stand in their new training centre and market, an extension of a Women's Garden, where they can harvest and sell saffron and vegetables, including these pickled varieties.

Fayzabad, Badakhshan, Afghanistan. **Maria de la Guardia, USA.** *Canon EOS 5D MkIII, 24-105mm lens, f4, 1/30s, ISO 500*

ONE SHOT 2015
WATER

Water is the essence of life on this planet. It is sustenance, growth, making up over 70% of our remarkable world as rivers, oceans, weather, floods, ice, presence or absence of water, tears; the list goes on.

In his winning image, Jasper Doest captures water sprayed over municipal waste in Marchena, Andalusia, Spain, transforming the grotesque excesses of man into a beautiful image of nature and light.

Sponsor of this award:
Photo Iconic

Marchena, Andalusia, Spain. **Jasper Doest, Netherlands.** *Canon EOS 100D, 400mm lens, f11, 1/1000s, ISO 400*

ONE SHOT 2015
WATER

Jasper Doest Netherlands
Winner

Previous Page. A black kite flies above as a stork stands on the ground while water is sprayed over the waste at a landfill site in order to dilute the acids that are being released during the decomposition of the waste.

ONE SHOT 2015
WATER

Stephan Fürnrohr Germany
Runner Up

Below. The sky, clouds and a trace of the midnight sun all mirrored in the bow wave of a small boat.

Near Ilulissat, Disko Bay, Greenland. **Stephan Fürnrohr, Germany.** *Nikon D800E, 24-70mm lens, f22, 1s, ISO 280*

ONE SHOT 2015
WATER

Wade Hughes Australia
Highly Commended

Right. A whale's eye perspective of a whale-watching boat as the skipper speaks by phone to lookouts perched on the high slopes of Pico Island.

Open sea off Pico Island in the Azores. **Wade Hughes, Australia.** *Canon 5D MkII, 35mm lens, f13, 1/200s, ISO 200*

ONE SHOT 2015
WATER

Joel Santos Portugal
Commended

Right. A salt miner takes a camel caravan on the lengthy trek to the mining site where the salt is cut by hand. This method of transporting salt has been used for centuries.

Salt flats, Afar region, Danakil Depression, Ethiopia. **Joel Santos, Portugal.** *Canon EOS 5D MkIII, 70-200mm lens, F4, 1/200s, ISO 200*

NEW TALENT 2015
STREET CULTURE

The art and craft of visual story telling is an essential part of photography and is fundamental for up and coming photographers to master.

Zhu Jingyi's intimate and engaging portfolio of life in Jiangsu, China, shows us the real people in their places of work. The expressions and the splashes of colour really make the portfolio stand out and come alive with intimacy and humour.

Sponsors of this award:

Plastic Sandwich, Photo Iconic, TPOTY

Jiangsu, China. **Zhu Jingyi, China.** *Nikon D800, 35mm lens, f8, 1/250s, ISO 100*

Jiangsu, China. **Zhu Jingyi, China.** *Nikon D800, 35mm lens, f8, 1/250s, ISO 100*

NEW TALENT 2015
STREET CULTURE

Zhu Jingyi China
Winner

Previous page: Mrs Liu is the seventh generation to teach in this school. Although she is over 90, and there are better living standards in the city, she refuses to leave because there are so many memories here.

Jiangsu, China. **Zhu Jingyi, China.** *Nikon D800, 35mm lens, f8, 1/250s, ISO 100*

Jiangsu, China. **Zhu Jingyi, China.** *Nikon D800, 35mm lens, f8, 1/250s, ISO 100*

Jiangsu, China. **Zhu Jingyi, China.** *Nikon D800, 35mm lens, f8, 1/250s, ISO 100*

Opposite page: A Chinese pancake master. The intense heat they have to endure at this moment is unbearable, even at top speed.

Above: On a morning in early summer an old man smiles as he washes beans.

Top right: Mr. Chen has managed his clock and watch store for over 20 years on the old street.

Right centre: Master shoemaker Li of Yuxi has made shoes for nearly 60 years. His shoes attract large numbers of customers because of their beauty, comfort and durability.

Right: Ma Chunfang, a 70 year old blacksmith, has honed his skills over 60 years. His cutting tools enjoy an especially good reputation locally.

Jiangsu, China. **Zhu Jingyi, China.** *Nikon D800, 35mm lens, f8, 1/250s, ISO 100*

Fuzhou, Fujian province, China. **Wang Changshu, China.**
Nikon D700, 14-24mm lens, f3.5, 1/60s, ISO 800

Fuzhou, Fujian province, China. **Wang Changshu, China.**
Nikon D700, 14-24mm lens, f5, 1/10s, ISO 800

Fuzhou, Fujian province, China. **Wang Changshu, China.**
Nikon D700, 14-24mm lens, f5, 1/125s, ISO 1600

Fuzhou, Fujian province, China. **Wang Changshu, China.**
Nikon D700, 14-24mm lens, f4, 1/25s, ISO 1250

Fuzhou, Fujian province, China. **Wang Changshu, China.**
Nikon D700, 14-24mm lens, f4, 1/40s, ISO 1000

Fuzhou, Fujian province, China. **Wang Changshu, China.** *Nikon D700, 14-24mm lens, f6.3, 1/4s, ISO 800*

NEW TALENT 2015
STREET CULTURE

Wang Changshu China
Runner Up

Shang Xia Hang consists of two parallel streets connecting the bridge and Damiao Road. As the estuary of the Minjiang River, this area used to be a busy port in Fuzhou. 'Fuzhou and Minjiang,' a photo book by British photographer John Thompson, documents the life of the people in this area between 1870 and 1871, as I have done here. The residents living on these two streets have retained their traditional lifestyle. In 2014, this area was renovated to become a tourism spot.

NEW TALENT 2015
STREET CULTURE

Carlos Esteves, Portugal
Highly Commended

Bhaktapur, Nepal. **Carlos Esteves, Portugal.**
Canon EOS 5D MkIII, 24-105mm lens, f4, 1/800s, ISO 4000

Kathmandu, Nepal. **Carlos Esteves, Portugal.**
Canon EOS 5D MkIII, 24-105mm lens, f5.6, 1/125s, ISO 1000

Bhaktapur, Nepal. **Carlos Esteves, Portugal.** *Canon EOS 5D MkIII, 24-105mm lens, f5.6, 1/125s, ISO 400*

Bhaktapur, Nepal. **Carlos Esteves, Portugal.** *Canon EOS 5D MkIII, 24-105mm lens, f7.1, 1/640s, ISO 1600*

Bhaktapur, Nepal. **Carlos Esteves, Portugal.**
Canon EOS 5D MkIII, 24-105mm lens, f4.5, 1/320s, ISO 800

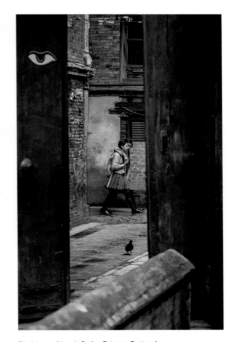

Bhaktapur, Nepal. **Carlos Esteves, Portugal.**
Canon EOS 5D MkIII, 24-105mm lens, f4, 1/500s, ISO 320

Glimpses of the ways of life for all generations can be found in the alleys of Kathmandu and Bhaktapur.

NEW TALENT 2015
STREET CULTURE

Yi Choon Tang, Malaysia
Commended

Kolkata is the first place I went to in India. I realised that the beauty of the culture can be discovered in different forms everywhere in India, even during busy working days.

Kolkata, India. **Yi Choon Tang, Malaysia.** *Nikon D750, 24-70mm lens, f5, 1/2500s, ISO 400*

Kolkata, India. **Yi Choon Tang, Malaysia.**
Nikon D750, 24-70mm lens, f11, 1/40s, ISO 100

Kolkata, India. **Yi Choon Tang, Malaysia.**
Nikon D750, 24-70mm lens, f7.1, 1/100s, ISO 400

Nusa Lembongan, Indonesia. **Alison Cahill, UK.**
Nikon D610, 50mm lens, f2.5, 1/125s, ISO 2500

Nusa Lembongan, Indonesia. **Alison Cahill, UK.**
Nikon D610, 50mm lens, f5.6, 1/200s, ISO 4000

NEW TALENT 2015
STREET CULTURE

Alison Cahill, UK
Commended

Dona is a tattoo artist from Nusa Lembongan, a small Hindu island located southeast of Bali. He is literally covered from head to foot in tattoos. Over recent years tattoos have become an increasingly popular fashion statement with young Balinese men.

Nusa Lembongan, Indonesia. **Alison Cahill, UK.** *Nikon D610, 50mm lens, f1.8, 1/125s, ISO 1600*

SMART SHOT 2015
iCAPTURED

The cameras on smartphones and tablets give an instant image, a response to an environment or an event. Their universal acceptance makes them less uncomfortable to the subject of an image.

Edgard de Bono's image captures the instant documentary nature of the medium but is also strikingly composed, giving a real sense of the presence of the photographer as an observer of what's happening in the world around us - the essence of good smartphone or tablet photography.

Sponsor of this award:
TPOTY

Benin City, Nigeria. **Edgard de Bono, Italy.** *iPhone 5s, f2.2, 1/800s, ISO 32*

Dresden, Germany. **Junjie Zeng, China.** *iPhone 5s, f2.2, 1/400s, ISO 32*

SMART SHOT 2015
iCAPTURED

Edgard de Bono Italy
Winner

Previous page: I was walking along the streets of Benin City when my attention was caught by the voices of women and children. The Mass had just finished and people were pouring out of church.

SMART SHOT 2015
iCAPTURED

Junjie Zeng China
Runner Up

Above: The rooftop of the Max Planck Institute, which is a science research institute in Dresden, Germany.

Tokyo, Japan. **Frederic Fouchet, France.** *iPhone 4s, f2.8, 1/60s, ISO 100*

San Diego, California, USA. **Pamelyn Chee, Singapore.** *iPhone 6, f2.2, 1/40s, ISO 125*

SMART SHOT 2015
iCAPTURED

Frederic Fouchet France
Highly Commended

Left: The older lady is thoughtful, and the juxtaposition of the two faces gives the impression that she is recalling her youth.

SMART SHOT 2015
iCAPTURED

Pamelyn Chee Singapore
Commended

Above: When changing her son's diaper, this mother put him on the giant leaf fan because the ground was too hot.

SMART SHOT 2015
iCAPTURED

Timothy Allen UK
Commended

Left: Shohan, a Mongolian Kazakh nomad, sits in a ger with his hunting eagle.

Mongolia. **Timothy Allen, UK.** *Nokia Lumia 1020, f2.2, 1/30s, ISO 125*

BEST SINGLE IMAGE
IN A PORTFOLIO 2015

Each year there are many portfolio entries which don't win prizes but amongst these are outstanding individual images. The best are selected from the portfolio by the judging panel and awarded the best single image in a portfolio or a judges' special mention. In 2015 these images were chosen from the three categories - Nature & Environment, Faces, People, Encounters and Monochromal.

Sponsor of this award:

Genesis Imaging

Western Mongolia. **Timothy Allen, UK.** *Canon 5D MkII, 50mm lens, f1.2, 1/8000s, ISO 100*

BEST SINGLE IMAGE
FACES, PEOPLE, ENCOUNTERS

Timothy Allen, UK
Winner

Previous page. Kazakh nomadic weddings involve a marriage ceremony and the obligatory wedding DJ but also horse racing, a wrestling tournament and copious amounts of prepared food and drink served in the family's gers.

BEST SINGLE IMAGE
FACES, PEOPLE, ENCOUNTERS

Ly Hoang Long, Vietnam
Special Mention

After the harvest crop, the villagers spend most of their time weaving these bamboo fishing baskets.

Tat Vien village, Hung Yen Province, Vietnam. **Ly Hoang Long, Vietnam.** *Nikon D4, 80-200mm lens, f10, 1/800s, ISO 640*

BEST SINGLE IMAGE
FACES, PEOPLE, ENCOUNTERS

Gianluca de Bartolo, Italy
Special Mention

Just before a ceremony, a young Orthodox priest is in a reflective mood on a foggy day.

Maramures, Romania. **Gianluca de Bartolo, Italy.** *Nikon D700, 17-35mm lens, f5, 1/160s, ISO 400*

BEST SINGLE IMAGE
FACES, PEOPLE, ENCOUNTERS

Beniamino Pisati, Italy
Special Mention

That February it was unusually cold, and the light was very soft. I discovered, returning to Cuba this year, that the two people portrayed are mother and son.

Trinidad, Cuba. **Beniamino Pisati, Italy.** *Canon 5D MkIII, 24-70mm lens, f4.5, 1/80s, ISO 2000*

BEST SINGLE IMAGE
FACES, PEOPLE, ENCOUNTERS

Allison Jonas Cardoso Gontijo, Brazil
Special Mention

Local children practice football, playing with the dream of
becoming professional players, all framed by a broken TV.

São Francisco, Minas Gerais, Brazil. **Alisson Jonas Cardoso Gontijo, Brazil.** *Canon 5D MkII, 24-70mm lens, f3.2, 1/600s, ISO 50*

Varanasi, India. **Gary Pullar, Australia.** *Olympus OMD-EM1, 14-35mm lens, f2, 1/4000s, ISO 250*

BEST SINGLE IMAGE
FACES, PEOPLE, ENCOUNTERS

Gary Pullar, Australia
Special Mention

The doms from the Untouchable caste, who manage the cremation process at Varanasi's largest crematorium, clamber over the remnants of discarded shrouds from the dead.

Omorate, Ethiopia. **Rafal Ziejewski, Poland.** *Canon EOS 5D MkII, 85mm lens, f2.5, 1/640s, ISO 200*

BEST SINGLE IMAGE
FACES, PEOPLE, ENCOUNTERS

Rafal Ziejewski, Poland
Special Mention

A young Dassenach girl. Dassenach live where the Omo
River delta enters Lake Turkana. Despite the lake and delta,
this is a very dry region, where daytime temperatures hover
around 35 degrees Centigrade.

Appenzell Alps, Switzerland. **Alessandra Meniconzi, Switzerland.** *Canon EOS 5D MkIII, 24-70mm lens, f16, 1/1328s, ISO 640*

BEST SINGLE IMAGE
NATURE & ENVIRONMENT

Alessandra Meniconzi, Switzerland
Winner

The impressive flight skills of the Alpine Chough.

BEST SINGLE IMAGE
NATURE & ENVIRONMENT

Georg Popp, Austria
Special Mention

Cypress swamp in Autumn.

Atchafalaya Basin, Louisiana, USA. **Georg Popp, Austria.** *Nikon D810, 70-200mm lens, f22, 1.6s, ISO 250*

Little Karoo, South Africa. **Brigitta Moser, Austria.** *Nikon D800, 300mm lens, f2.8, 1/2000s, ISO 800*

BEST SINGLE IMAGE
NATURE & ENVIRONMENT

Brigitta Moser, Austria
Special Mention

The best way to see meerkats is in the early morning when they come out of their underground caves and warm up in the sun.

Terry Steeley, UK
Special Mention

Sunset split of a large lemon shark cruising the ocean surface.

Tiger Beach, Bahamas. **Terry Steeley, UK.** *Canon 1DX, 8-15mm fisheye lens, f11, 1/160s, ISO 320*

Anette Mossbacher, Germany
Special Mention

This polar bear was on the hunt for seals. He covered the whole island within an hour without finding any seals between the rocks.

Nordenskiöld glacier, Adolfbukta, Svalbard, Norway. **Anette Mossbacher, Germany.** *Canon 1DX, 70-200mm lens, f8, 1/400s, ISO 400*

Tonga, South Pacific. **Scott Portelli, Australia.** *Canon EOS 5D Mk III, 15mm fisheye lens, f8, 1/320s, ISO 320*

BEST SINGLE IMAGE
MONOCHROMAL

Scott Portelli, Australia
Winner

After a young whale calf explores its environment by launching its three-ton body out of the water, a jetstream of bubbles is produced as the calf re-enters the liquid atmosphere like a rocket.

BEST SINGLE IMAGE
MONOCHROMAL

Timothy Allen, UK
Winner

A young boy sleeps on a huge pile of cardboard amidst the rubbish of Kibarani refuse dump on the outskirts of Mombasa, Kenya.

Kibarani waste dump, Mombasa, Kenya. **Timothy Allen, UK.** *Canon 5D MkII, 16-35mm lens, f2.8, 1/160s, ISO 640*

Antarctica. **Scott Portelli, Australia.**
Canon EOS 5D MkIII, 100-400mm lens, f20, 1/250s, ISO 250

BEST SINGLE IMAGE
MONOCHROMAL

Scott Portelli, Australia
Special Mention

A Weddell seal rests peacefully on the frozen landscape in Antarctica.

BEST SINGLE IMAGE
MONOCHROMAL

Thierry Bornier, France
Special Mention

An ethnic Yi child, living in one of the most poverty-stricken regions of China.

Liangshan, Sichuan, China. **Thierry Bornier, France.**
Nikon D800E, 70-200mm lens, f4, 1/250s, ISO 400

Rajasthan, India. **Stuart Redler, UK.** *Mamiya RZ67, 110mm lens, f11, 1/125, ISO 320*

BEST SINGLE IMAGE
MONOCHROMAL

Stuart Redler UK
Special Mention

Friends attempting to ride five to a moped.

BEST SINGLE IMAGE
MONOCHROMAL

Alessandra Meniconzi, Switzerland
Special Mention

Switzerland is a camelid paradise, due to the weather and altitude.

Appenzell, Switzerland. **Alessandra Meniconzi, Switzerland.** *Canon EOS 5D MkIII, 70-200mm lens, f8, 1/1328s, ISO 640*

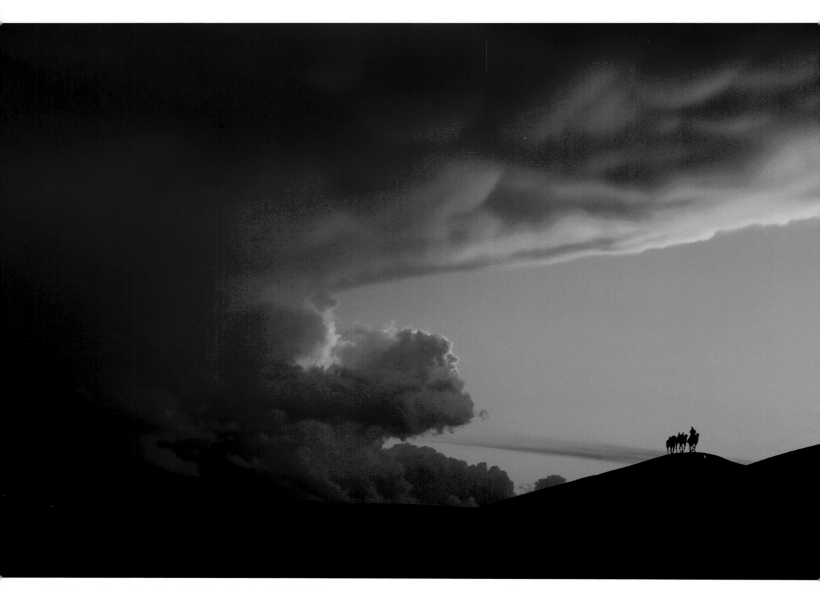

Camels at sunset. Neyman, Inner Mongolia. **Li Yushan, China.** *Canon EOS 5D MkIII, 28-300mm lens, f8, 1/40s. ISO 100*

JUDGES

The TPOTY judging panel is international and made up of experts from the world of photography and travel. They are selected to reflect a variety of backgrounds, styles and attitudes to photography and the photographic image. A key element of the panel is the wealth of visual and specialist expertise brought into the mix by our technical and creative judges. Lay judges and past winners have also participated, bringing fresh views and perspectives to the judging process.

These judges give their time because they are passionate about photography, and we are immensely grateful for their efforts.

We would like to thank the 2015 judging panel:

Judges

Daria Bonera - *photo agency director and photo editor for National Geographic Traveller, Italy*

Barbara Bordnick - *photographer and lecturer*

Catherine Capon - *adventurer, naturalist, wildlife filmmaker and environmental activist*

Chris Coe - *photographer, author & lecturer*

Richard Dunwoody - *champion jockey, adventurer and travel photographer*

Jeremy Hoare - *photographer & TV cameraman*

Debbie Ireland - *picture editor & curator*

Brigitte Lardinois - *curator & academic*

Eamonn McCabe - *award-winning photographer & picture editor*

Caroline Metcalfe - *former director of photography, Condé Nast Traveller*

Michael Pritchard - *Director-General, The Royal Photographic Society*

Mary Robert - *Head of Photography, Richmond, the American International University in London*

Jerry Tavin - *stock photography expert and founder of Young Photographers' Alliance*

Emma Thomson - *award-winning travel writer*

Chris Weston - *wildlife photographer*

Manfred Zollner - *photographic critic and deputy editor in chief, Fotomagazin, Germany*

Fishing nets at Tuyen Lam lake, Vietnam. **Ly Hoang Long, Vietnam.** *D700, 24-70mm lens, f10, 15sec, ISO 200*

SPONSORS AND PARTNERS

FUJIFILM

Fujifilm

Fujifilm is a global leader in imaging technology, products and services including digital cameras, photofinishing, digital storage and recording media, consumer and professional film, motion picture film, professional video, printing systems, medical imaging, office technology, flat panel displays and graphic arts. The company employs more than 73,000 people worldwide, with 178 subsidiaries stretching across four continents. In the UK, Fujifilm has been supplying the imaging, printing and graphics industries, as well as consumers, professional and enthusiast photographers, with high quality, innovative products and services for over 25 years. Fujifilm UK currently employs more than 400 people and has become one of the country's most popular photographic and imaging brands. All the TPOTY exhibition prints are produced on Fujifilm Crystal Archive paper.
www.fujifilm.eu/uk

Páramo Directional Clothing

One of the most innovative brands in the mountain, travel and exploration market, Páramo has provided high performance technical clothing for all environments for 20+ years, combining uniquely directional Nikwax fabrics and ingenious, practical designs. Páramo is the leading clothing of choice for Mountain Rescue Teams and expeditionary workforces such as the British Antarctic Survey, as well as being the preference of many photography and nature professionals travelling all over the globe. In January 2016, ethically-manufactured Páramo became the first outdoor clothing company to sign up to Greenpeace's Detox commitment, ensuring hazardous and polluting chemicals are excluded from clothing manufacture.
www.paramo-clothing.com

Hurtigruten

An exploration company in the truest sense of the word, Hurtigruten have been embarking on journeys of discovery and authentic adventure for 123 years. Our fleet of 14 ships embark on 50 unique routes to visit some of the most unexplored and pristine coasts across 19 countries. On a voyage with Hurtigruten, you can expect real experiences that bring you closer to the landscapes and the local communities that we visit.
www.hurtigruten.co.uk

StaaG®

StaaG® is a British lifestyle brand. The brand was founded by two Scottish brothers who grew up with design from a young age and British traditions in their DNA. StaaG® offers uniqueness and quality allowing you to demonstrate your appetite for exclusivity and an understanding of the traditionally modern British lifestyle. The StaaG product range includes ready to wear premium polo shirts, British handmade leather goods, sterling silver accessories and other related products.
www.staag.co

SPONSORS AND PARTNERS

Plastic Sandwich

Plastic Sandwich was founded in the early 1970s by Joyce Pinto. Rob Jacobs joined the company 5 years later. The service provides a complete portfolio presentation package for photographers, designers and ad agencies. Plastic Sandwich has had unparalleled experience in the field of image presentation in its various forms over the last 40 years and we have been the proud sponsors of the TPOTY competition since 2003. Plastic Sandwich's services are also utilised by companies such as event and PR organisations, film companies, high-end presenters, and anyone whose activities or craft are best shown through the presentation of images. We are now an affiliate company to Jaguar Land Rover.
www.plasticsandwich.co.uk

SNAPP Guides

SNAPP Guides is a photography location finding app for iOS and Android that offers a collection of high quality destination guides for the travelling photographer. These interactive guides will help you discover incredible new places to photograph, plus provide inspiration and creative ideas once you get there. The SNAPP Guides app uses the latest map technology, accurate GPS coordinates, ideal times and conditions, itinerary planning tools, and includes plenty of invaluable advice to help you photograph like a local from the minute you arrive.
www.snappguides.co

> We would like to thank the TPOTY sponsors
> for their support, without which
> the awards would not be possible.

Direct Photographic

With offices in London, Paris and Cape Town, Direct Photographic is dedicated to delivering the very best in rental equipment to photographers Worldwide. An active supporter of the industry as a whole, Direct Photographic is a keen investor in the latest equipment and remains committed to helping capture the vision of both emerging and established photographers.
www.directphotographic.co.uk

Genesis Imaging

One of the UK's leading providers of photographic and fine art printing and finishing services, Genesis Imaging is in the unique position of providing a comprehensive range of photographic printing, mounting and framing services to some of the best-known photographers, artists and art galleries around, people who demand the very best quality available. Our superb photographic prints, mounts and frames have graced the walls of famous galleries from London's National Portrait Gallery to New York's Museum of Modern Art.
www.genesisimaging.co.uk

Photo Iconic

Photo Iconic offers a range of TPOTY photography courses and workshops, masterclasses, international photographic adventures and private tuition to suit all abilities and styles of photography - tutored by award-winning photographers.
www.photoiconic.com.

Dolphins and freediver, White Sand Ridge, Little Bahama Banks, The Bahamas. **Laura Storm, UK.** *Canon EOS 550D, 15mm lens, f7.1, 1/640mm, ISO 200*

Snail, San Miniato, Pisa, Italy. **Stefano Coltelli, Italy.** *Nikon D600, 210mm lens, f14, 1/100sec, ISO 400*

INDEX OF PHOTOGRAPHERS

We would like to thank the photographers whose images appear in this book. Their support, along with that of all the other photographers from across the world who enter the awards, makes the Travel Photographer of the Year awards and this book possible.

Allen, Timothy	*24, 28, 29, 83, 85, 97*
Berman, Hugo	*23*
Bornier, Thierry	*98*
Cahill, Alison	*79*
Cai, Zhiping	*Front cover, 59*
Chee, Pamelyn	*83*
Cole, Trevor	*4*
Coltelli, Stefano	*106*
Cox, Spencer	*12, 16, 17*
de Bartolo, Gianluca	*87*
de Bono, Edgard	*81*
de la Guardia, Maria	*65*
Doest, Jasper	*67*
Esteves, Carlos	*76, 77*
Fouchet, Frederic	*83*
Francolini, Andrea	*5*
Fürnrohr, Stephan	*68, Back cover*
Ghose, Victor	*22*
Golden, Piers	*3, 62*
Guttman, Chase	*13, 14, 15*
Harvey, Philip Lee	*48, 49*
Hughes, Wade	*69*
Jianhui, Liao	*42, 43*
Jonas Cardoso Gontijo, Allison	*88*
Junjie, Zeng	*82*
Kanashkevich, Mitchell	*25, 26, 27, Back cover*
Kunz, Uli	*55, Back cover*
Louie, Larry	*50, 51, 61*
Li, Yushan	*100*
Ly, Hoang Long	*86, 102*
Meniconzi, Alessandra	*34, 91, 99*
Mingorance, Francisco	*38, 39*
Morgan, James	*35, 36, 37*
Moser, Brigitta	*93*
Mossbacher, Anette	*95*
O'Connell, Sue	*30, 31*
Palacios, Ignacio,	*63*
Pisati, Beniamino	*87*
Popp, George	*92*
Portelli, Scott	*44, 96, 98*
Pullar, Gary	*89*
Redler, Stuart	*32, 33, 99*
Rystrøm, Johnathan	*18, 19*
Santos, Joel	*69*
Scharf, Ido	*23*
Steeley, Terry	*94*
Storm, Laura	*105*
Streu, Gunar	*Frontispiece, 58*
Tan, Adam	*52, 53*
Tang, Yi Choon	*78*
Taylor, Tim	*57*
Theodric, Michael	*20, 21*
van Oosten, Marsel	*6, 7, 8, 9, 10, 11, Back cover*
Vekemans, Ingrid	*40, 41*
Wang, Changshu	*74, 75*
Wrangborg, David	*56*
Xia, Xuejun	*44, 45, 46, 47*
Ziejewski, Rafal	*90*
Zhou, Jianyong	*64*
Zhu, Jingyi	*70, 71, 72, 73*

TAKE ANOTHER JOURNEY, JOIN US ON ANOTHER ADVENTURE.

Journey One
2003-04

Journey Two
2005-06

Journey Three
2007-08

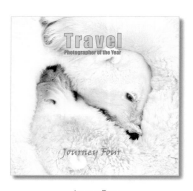

Journey Four
2010-11

Journey Five
2012

Journey Six
2013

Journey Seven
2014

Travel Photographer of the Year Collection

Visit www.tpoty.com to buy Journeys One to Eight. Many of the award-winning images from Travel Photographer of the Year are also available as postcards, greeting cards and exhibition quality prints in the Travel Photographer of the Year Collection, available from our online shop.

The photographers receive royalties from the sale of their images. Enter TPOTY for a chance to see your photography published in a future Journey portfolio book at www.tpoty.com